NATE'S NOISY NOSE

Hey adults!
When you read the story to your kids, ask them to shout out the sound words after you say them!
This is a **NOISY** book!

Published by Frances Mackay 2024
www.francesmackay.com
Text Copyright © Frances Mackay 2024
Illustration Copyright © Dotti Colvin 2024
Design by Nicky Scott
www.nickyscottdesign.com
Editor Lor Bingham
www.calicoediting.com
Creative Consultant Stacey Gittens
www.faithfulstories.com

The moral right of the author has been asserted.
All rights reserved. No part of this book may be reproduced or transmitted
by any person or entity, including Internet search engines or retailers, in any form
or any means, electronic or mechanical, including photocopying (except under statutory
exceptions provisions of the Australian Copyright Act 1968), recording, scanning or by
any information storage and retrieval system without prior written
permission of Frances Mackay, author.

A catalogue record for this book is available from the National Library of Australia

ISBN 978-0-646-70532-3

NATE'S NOISY NOSE

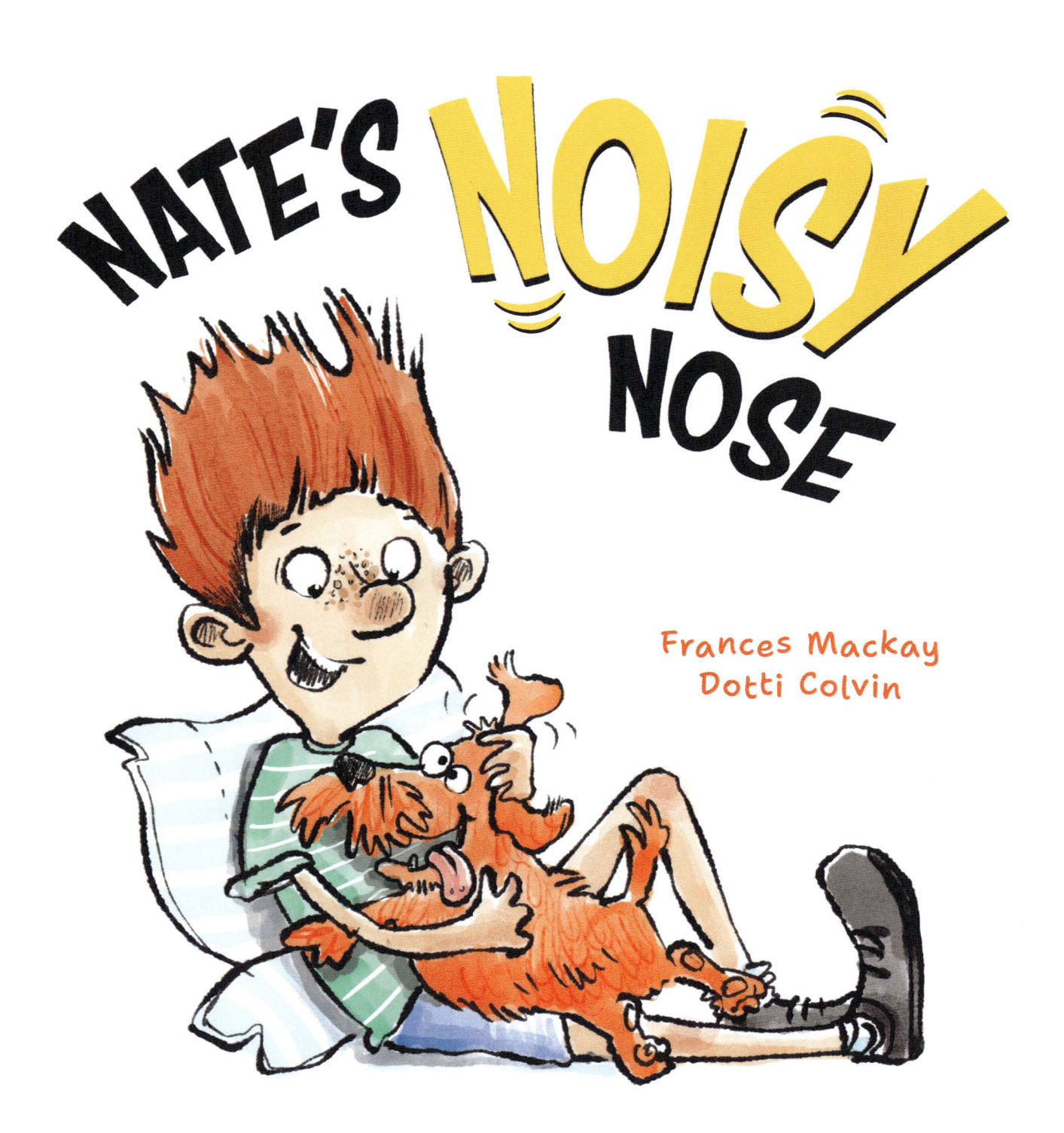

Frances Mackay
Dotti Colvin

There are all kinds of noses.

little noses

BIG noses

warty noses

SPOTTY NOSES

SNOTTY NOSES

red noses

NARROW NOSES

Wide noses

BUMPY NOSES

FINGER-PICKING NOSES

And then there's...

...the nose of Nate Tyler-Jones.

It looks quite normal, doesn't it? Just like any other nose.

But take a **closer** look.

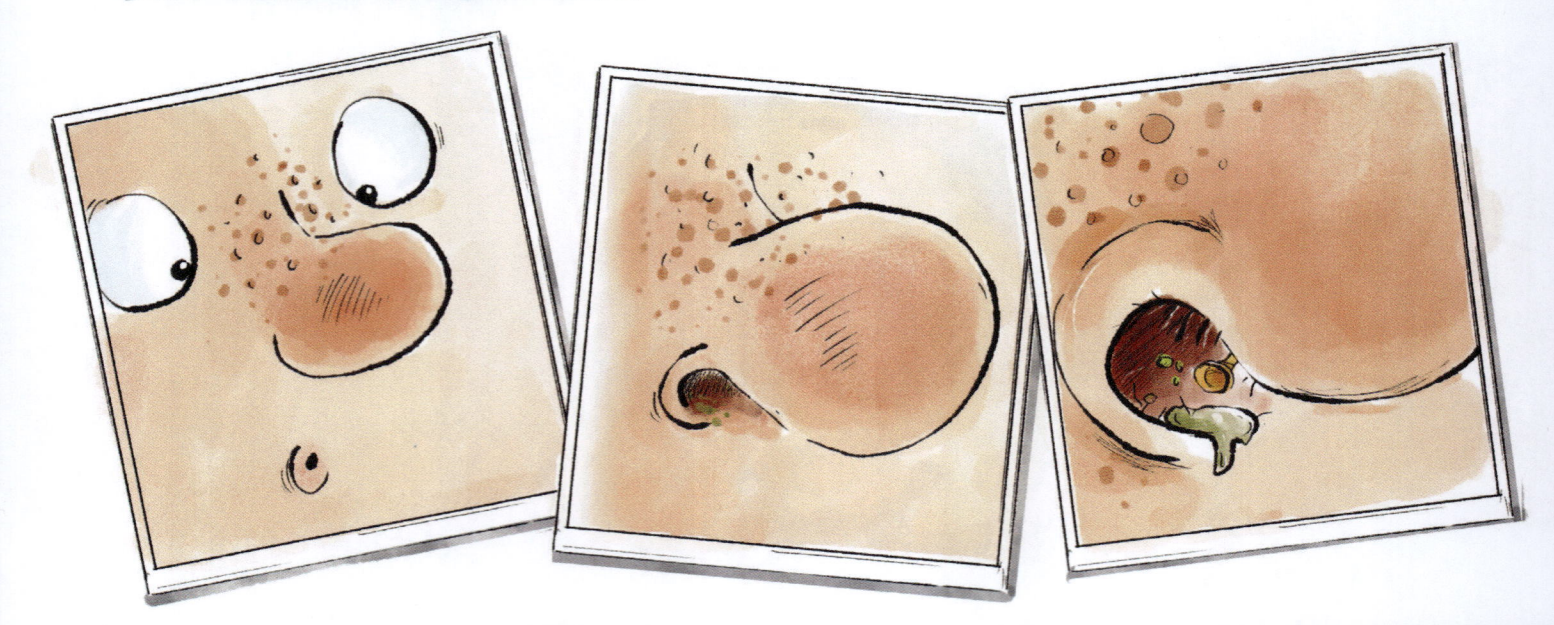

What do you see?

No one had a nose like Nate's.

It made all kinds of **musical** sounds.

Nate thought it was something special.
And so did his dog, Rascal.

He made his friends laugh.

He protected the veggie patch.

He made music with Rascal.

But there was a problem.
A **BIG** problem.

Nate's nose was **NOISY!**
It caused him problems at home.

TOOT! TOOT! RING! RING!

His brother couldn't sleep.

No one could hear the TV.

WHISTLE! WHISTLE! PLINK! PLINK!

And the noise terrified the cat!

The family tried to find solutions.

But they couldn't hear each other.

They gave Nate his own room, but he wanted to be with his brother.

They made a hiding place for the cat, but everyone missed her cuddles.

Not me! Hee hee!

Nate's nose caused problems at school.
In the classroom...

...at choir practice...

...and in the library.

TWINGLE! TWINGLE! TICKA! TICKA!

So, his best friend tried to fix it!

Nate's nose caused chaos in the neighbourhood.
In the shopping mall...

CLANG! CLANG!
BOOM! BOOM!

...at the cinema...

...and at the zoo.

So people took action!

And soon, Nate wasn't welcome anywhere.

NO NATES ALLOWED!!

ZOO

Nate's family decided it was time to look for help. They took him to every nose specialist they could find. Nate's nose was examined by highly qualified doctors and top scientists.

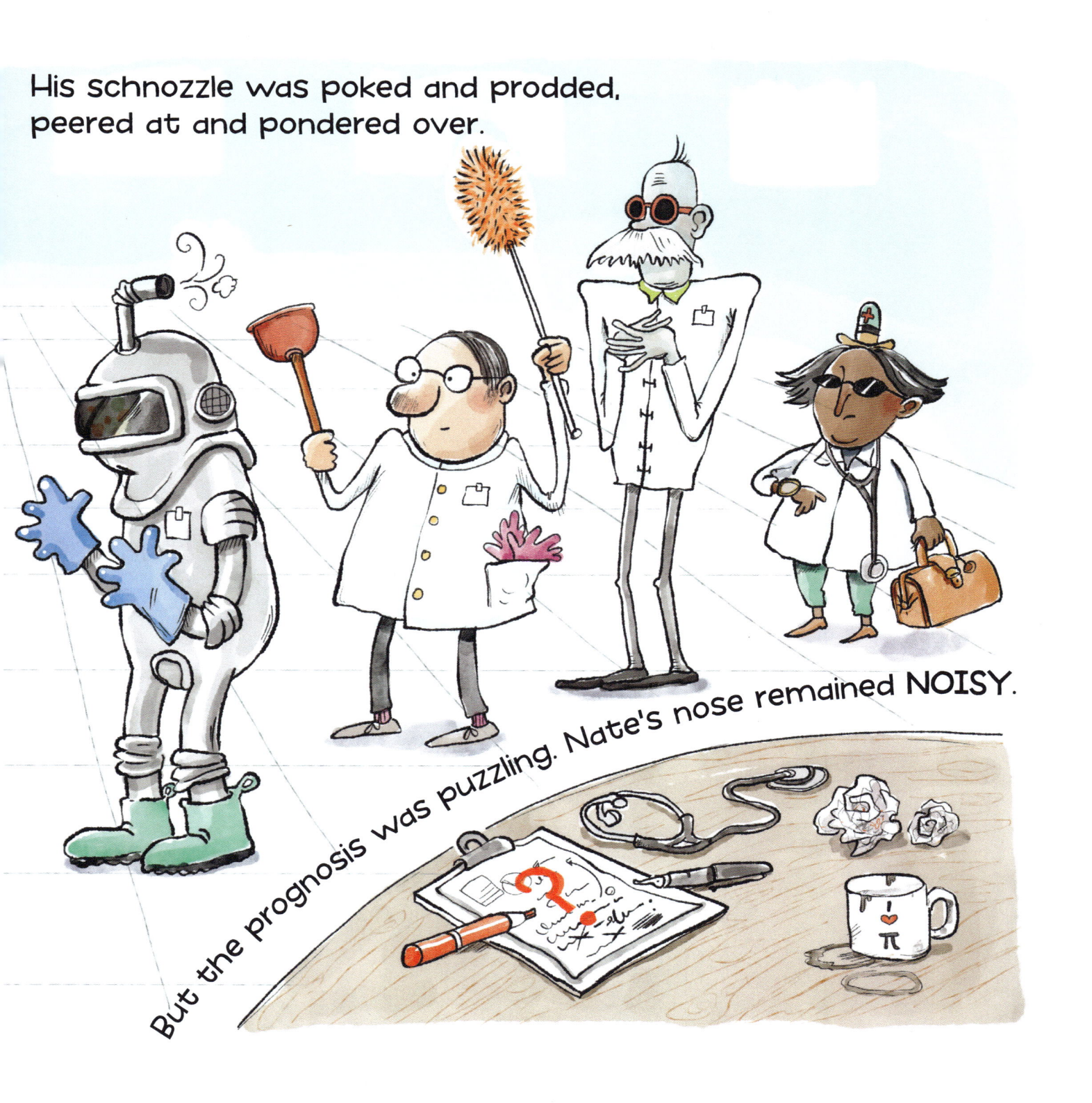

His schnozzle was poked and prodded, peered at and pondered over.

But the prognosis was puzzling. Nate's nose remained NOISY.

Nate didn't think his nose was special anymore, so he tried to fix it himself.

He taped his nostrils together.

He wore his snorkelling mask.

He put his head in a bucket.

But nothing muffled the noise. Eventually, he just hid himself away, so he wouldn't upset anyone.

One day, there was a knock at the door, and there stood Gabby the Geek, the world-famous electronics wizard!

She had heard about Nate's nose and was determined to solve the problem.

Gabby tinkered and tampered, tightened and tested.

Finally, she came up with the
NOISY
NOSE
MACHINE!

All she had to do was turn it ON!

There was buzzing and beeping, pinging and popping.

Nate felt a tickle in his nose.
Just a little tickle at first.
He wiggled his nose and waited.

Then the tickle GREW,
and GREW,
and GREW,
and GREW,

until...

AAAACHOOOOOOOOO!

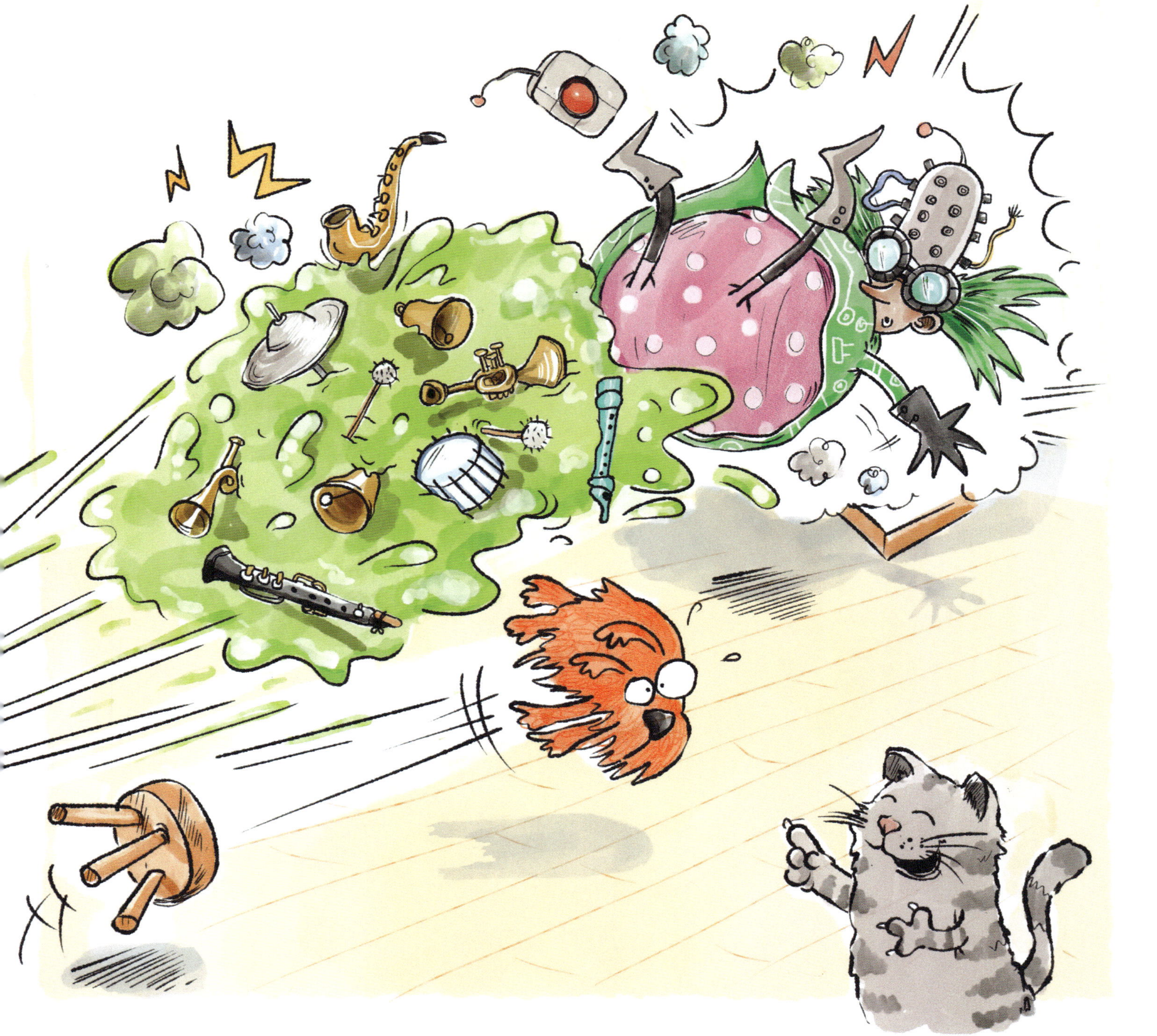

Rascal saw the pile of gooey, snotty stuff on the floor. Before Nate could stop him, Rascal had gobbled it all up!

BURP!!

Rascal ran to Nate and let out a happy '**woof**', but it wasn't a woof at all!
It was a...

WAH! WAH!
OOM-PAH-PAH!

Oh no!
What a disaster!

Or was it?

Nate loved his quiet nose, but it didn't stop him, or Rascal, from making a LOT of NOISE!

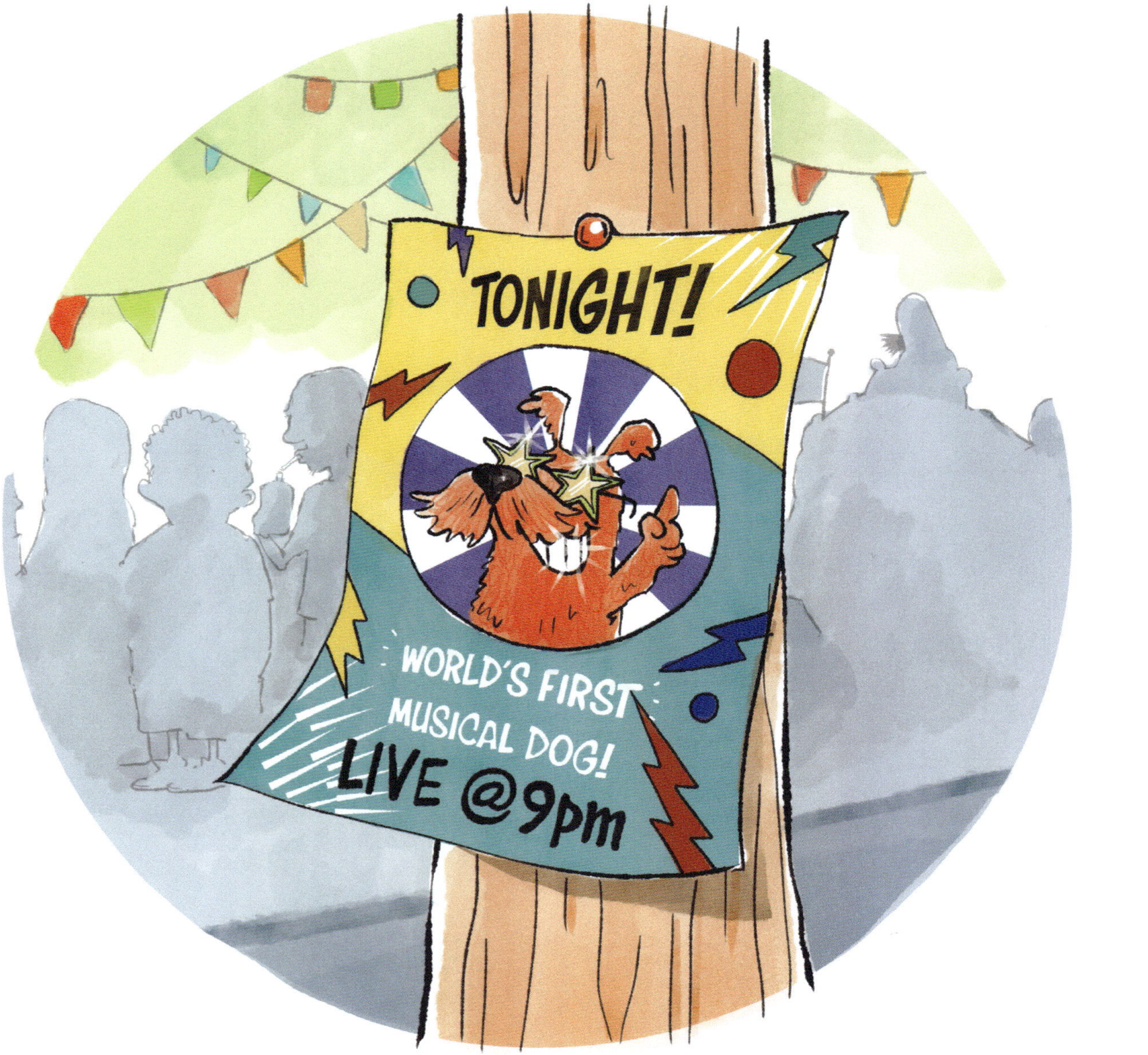
TONIGHT!
WORLD'S FIRST
MUSICAL DOG!
LIVE @9pm

ABOUT THE AUTHOR

Frances Mackay is the author of more than 90 teacher resource books and has written several picture books, activity books and information books.

She was a primary school teacher for 20 years in Australia and the UK. She loves writing books that make learning fun!

facebook:
@francesmackaychildrensauth
or
instagram:
@frances.mackay_author

ABOUT THE ILLUSTRATOR

Dotti Colvin has been an animator and cartoonist for 20 years, working in London, Brighton and New York in the area of TV advertising and more recently editorial and print media.
Born in the UK and now living in Italy, her work reflects her approachable and humorous nature and never fails to raise a smile.

DID YOU ENJOY THIS BOOK?

Your feedback helps me provide the best quality books and helps other readers like you discover great books.

You can leave a review online or send it direct to me at: frances@francesmackay.com

I read and appreciate each one.

Thank You! ☺

Read more about Frances & grab some FREEBIES at: www.francesmackay.com

BOOKS BY FRANCES MACKAY
www.francesmackay.com

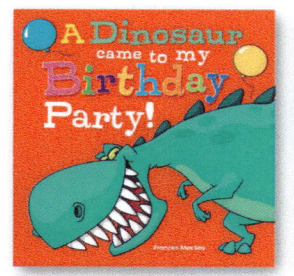

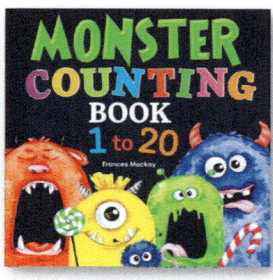

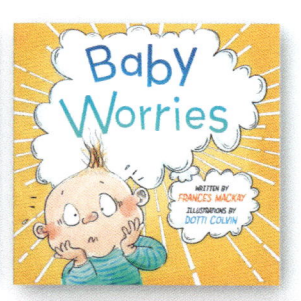

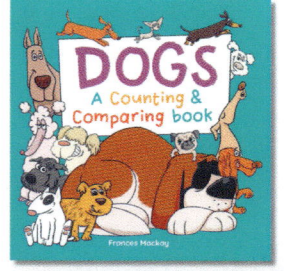

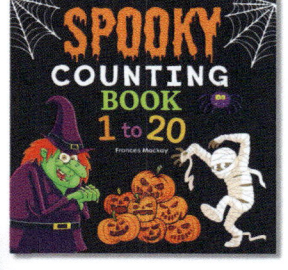

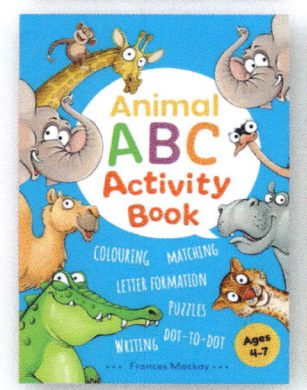

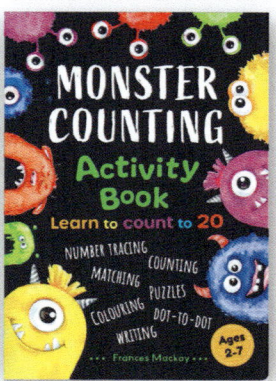

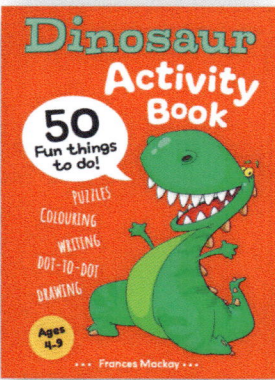

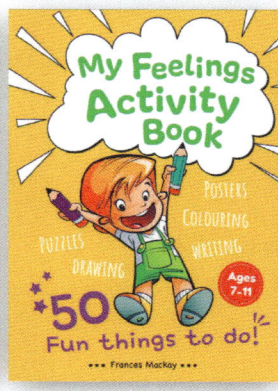

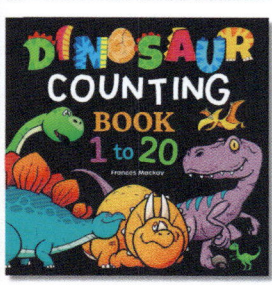

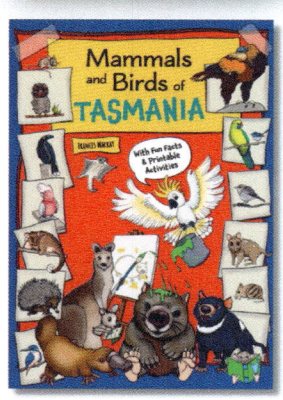

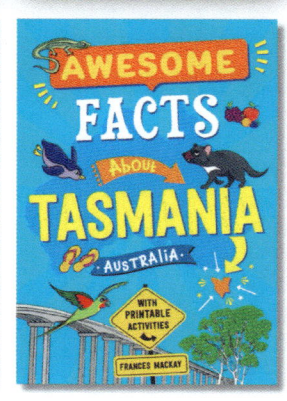

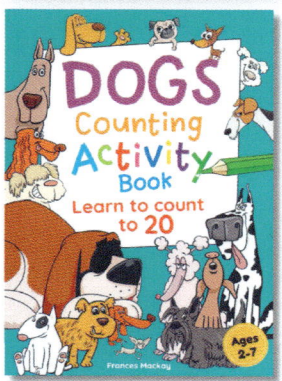

Reading and learning should be a fun experience for children. Our books have been created to excite children's curiosity, creativity and imagination.

Printed in Great Britain
by Amazon